RED FLAGS:
DON'T IGNORE THEM

Volume 1

Hazel-Ann Pariag

Michael Terence Publishing

First published in paperback by
Michael Terence Publishing in 2019
www.mtp.agency

Copyright © 2019 Hazel-Ann Pariag
hazel-annfullhundred1@live.com

Hazel-Ann Pariag has asserted the right to be identified as the
author of this work in accordance with the
Copyright, Designs and Patents Act 1988

ISBN 9781913289348

No part of this publication may be reproduced, stored in a retrieval
system, or transmitted, in any form or by any means, electronic,
mechanical, photocopying, recording or otherwise, without the prior
permission of the publishers

Cover images
Copyright © Hazel-Ann Pariag, Macrovector, Fastfun23

Cover design
Copyright © 2019 Michael Terence Publishing

Dedication

This book is dedicated to any adult, male or female, who is seeking a partner in marriage. Although the Holy Bible can be considered, among other things, "The Marriage Manual", I truly believe I was inspired by Holy Ghost to write this book to be an aid in Marriage Counselling and to encourage persons to fully involve God in their marriage plans.

If your desire is to seek God and not lean on your own wisdom for marriage, then I gladly dedicate this book to you.

Acknowledgements

I wish to express with deep gratitude, thanks to Almighty God and my Saviour, Jesus Christ. Without God, I am nothing. All honour and glory go to God. On my own, I could not have written this book. Holy Spirit guided me all along.

I also wish to acknowledge those persons to whom Almighty God has given a measure of faith and who have been of great help to me. These individuals, some total strangers to one another, have each been role models to me. They have encouraged me to seek newer and deeper territories in Christ Jesus and a greater level of growth in his glory, anointing and power.

They have all been a great blessing to me. I have learned much from watching how they conduct themselves in their personal lives, in their ministry and how they walk in integrity.

Apostle Jemma Duncan and Pastor Celestine have been "mothers in the faith to me".

Minister Dana Charles has been a brother to me.

I do highly appreciate Mr Leonard Duncan and his team, Alicia and Anna, for their high quality of production in the printing and publishing of this book.

I pray God's richest blessings on you all!

Contents

Introduction 1
Our Official Meeting... 4
Blindness 8
Red Flag #1: Too Good to Be True.................................. 12
Red Flag #2: Traps.. 14
Red Flag #3: Obsessive Shadowing 18
Red Flag #4: The Ex-Syndrome 22
Red Flag #5: Moving In 25
Red Flag #6: Skeletons Coming Out of the Closet............ 28
Red Flag #7: Financial Issues 31
Red Flag #8: Siblings and In-Laws 35
Red Flag #9: Refusing Counsel....................................... 38
Red Flag #10: Colourful Lies 40
Red Flag #11: Sickness and More Lies 42
Red Flag #12: The Wedding.. 45

Life After the Wedding 48
A Prenuptial Checklist 50
Advice for the Starry-Eyed 52
Some Things to Consider or Avoid in Preparation for Marriage 54
Question to Self 61
My Support Group 62
Conclusion 65

Introduction

This book is based on my real-life experiences. It is Volume 1 of a two-volume series. In this book, you will read of some events that may make your jaw drop. Let me assure you that nothing was made up.

It is autobiographic, cross-referenced with scriptures, dealing with the matter of waiting on, and trusting God for a partner. We tend to proceed without seeking confirmation as to whether the person who comes along is the divinely-appointed partner sent by God; or, was (s)he just a distraction of the enemy?

You will read how leaning on your own understanding is a perfect recipe for disaster.

Proverbs 3:5-7

⁵Trust in the LORD with all thine heart; and lean not unto thine own understanding.

⁶In all thy ways acknowledge him, and he shall direct thy paths.

⁷Be not wise in thine own eyes: fear the LORD, and depart from evil.

Letting down your guard or disabling your discernment because you like someone is DANGEROUS. We must put on the whole armour of God, at all times.

God hates divorce, although the Bible gives grounds for it. Divorce and remarriage can, and should, be avoided at all costs.

Malachi 2:16 (NKJV)

16 For the LORD God of Israel says that He hates divorce, "For it covers one's garment with violence," says the LORD of hosts. "Therefore take heed to your spirit, That you do not deal treacherously."

It also says in Psalms 1, *"Blessed is the man who walks not in the counsel of the ungodly, nor stands in the way of sinners, nor sits in the seat of the scornful. But his delight is in the Law of the Lord, and on his Law he meditate day and night. He is like a tree planted by the rivers of water, that brings forth fruit in its season, and his leaf does not wither. In all that he does, he prospers. The ungodly are not so: but are like the chaff the wind drives away. Therefore, the ungodly shall not stand in the judgement, nor sinners of the righteous, for the Lord knows the way of the righteous, but the way of the ungodly shall perish."*

The man who meditates on the law of the Lord is like a tree planted by rivers of water - alive, thriving, strong and mighty. We need to take our thoughts captive and replace them with the Word of God. We need to condition our minds to respond in a godly fashion in times of temptation, rather than be impatient.

"Do not be conformed to this world, but be transformed by the renewing of our mind, that by testing you may discern what is the will of God, what is good and acceptable and perfect." Romans 12:2.

How do we do this? Philippians 4:8 recommends we meditate on commendable things. We must meditate on God and His word, His handiwork and majesty and on His instructions. When we do this, we become sensitive to Holy Spirit's leading; we become more discerning and can pick up on the red flags, those warnings that would save us much heartache and personal disaster as we journey through life.

I made up my mind some time ago that if by sharing my story, I could help someone else avoid the mistakes that I made, then I must do so. This is the first part of that story. God, through His Holy Spirit, is forever trying to steer us away from danger and along His path of right living, but as is so often the case, we ignore the red flags - the signs, the prompts and warnings - signalling danger, especially if we want to have our own way, anyway.

I pray that as you read, you will be impressed to heed the signs before you and not ignore the red flags. Most importantly, I pray that you will be drawn ever closer to God, our Father, through our Lord and Saviour, Jesus Christ.

He cares so deeply about us and wants only the best for us, if we would only learn to trust Him all the way.

Our Official Meeting

It was around 10.30 a.m. that day. I was at work, had just finished my day's duty, and two female colleagues were literally nagging me to accompany them to Central City to window shop for curtains, so as to make up the time until 2 p.m. when our shift would end. The Hindu festival of Divali was coming up soon so there would have been a lot of bargains in the stores.

My colleagues got on the 11.00 o'clock bus and called me on my phone urging me to hurry as I was keeping back the bus which was already loaded. I was just passing the time in the lobby, so I decided that I would go. I hustled out to the platform and on to the waiting bus. My friends were almost down to the back and were calling out to me saying they had a seat for me. There were standing passengers, so I had to manoeuvre to get to the back.

When I got there, there was this man on the opposite side, literally wiping the seat with his rag for me to sit. My colleagues were laughing and saying something to him. I was not aware of what was happening or what conversation had taken place before I arrived, so I must have looked like Alice in Wonderland.

As we travelled, they explained what had transpired and I, too, had a good laugh. They had told this total stranger to put his backpack on the seat to show that it was occupied and told him a nice female was going to sit next to him. His response was, "I don't want any woman and I not looking for any." However, when he saw me walking down the aisle in the bus, he quickly took out his rag and began wiping the seat for me to sit.

On the journey, we spoke about things in general. When he observed that I was reading the Bible on my phone, he asked if I was a Christian. I told him I was, and a lot of other questions followed. Coincidentally, he knew a lot of people I also knew from a church that he said he was a member of. On reaching to Central City, we disembarked from the bus. He had tried to get my name and contact information before leaving, but I simply ignored him.

My colleagues, knowing I was single, started asking me if I had got his details. When they heard I hadn't, they went on and on asking, "So how you expect to meet someone, if you not giving anyone your name or number? They even added, "But the man is Christian like yourself and you all know people in common!" Of course, they had been listening in on our conversation!

Later that night, as usual, I was at home online on a particular social network when I saw a picture pop up. I looked at it saying to myself, "But that's the same person from the bus this morning," while taking a closer look at his picture and viewing his profile. I decided to message him asking, "Were you on a bus to Central this morning?" He responded, "Yes, and you were sitting right next to me!" The messaging continued. OMG, this seemed like a mystery! Was this really happening? This had to be God, I thought: meeting this person today for the second time, after parting without exchanging names or contact numbers!

That was the beginning of the relationship.

Hazel-Ann Pariag

Blindness

In my eyes he was all that I had prayed for: he had his own house, a permanent government job, he was living alone and had no children. James 1:14-15 reminds us, *"But every man is tempted, when he is drawn away of his own lust, and enticed. Then when lust hath conceived, it bringeth forth sin; and sin, when it is finished, bringeth forth death."* Boy, was I drawn away; was I enticed!

He had been praying for a wife and here I was single, renting an apartment and living on my own. I, too, was in a permanent government job. I had a grown child from another relationship, while he had three adopted "children": his pets - a parrot and two love birds. The match seemed ideal. It appears nothing could have ever possibly gone wrong.

Hazel-Ann Pariag

"But the Lord said unto Samuel: Look not on his countenance, or on the height of his stature; because I have refused him: for the LORD seeth; for man looketh on the outward appearance, but the LORD looketh on the heart 1 Samuel 16:7.

I must admit, I did just what God's word said not to do: I fell for the outward appearance, not seeing beneath the surface.

Hazel-Ann Pariag

RED FLAG WARNING ISSUED

Red Flag #1: Too Good to Be True

When I met him, he had been out of fellowship with His Lord and Saviour, Jesus Christ, and had been back-slidden for about seven years. Immediately after we began our relationship, he started going back to church with me. I was really happy about this. This was what I had always hoped for: a husband who would be head and head with me in church. We seemed to be the perfect match.

Let's face it, it is painfully obvious that I was immature spiritually and oh, so blinded by love! But I was soon to discover that all that glitters is not gold.

The fact that he was in a back-slidden state should have warned me that I was on potentially dangerous ground because we were unequally yoked. I subsequently discovered that he had been involved in common-law relationships and had been shacking up.

On reflection, I would admit his going back to church was good, but definitely not good enough. He needed deliverance, and to engage in repentance and renewing of his mind. There would have been soul ties and transference of spirits resulting from all his illicit relationships; but, naively, I had put myself at risk and I could have perished for lack of knowledge. But for God!

My people are destroyed for lack of knowledge: because thou hast rejected knowledge, I will also reject thee, that thou shalt be no priest to me: seeing thou hast forgotten the law of thy God, I will also forget thy children. Hosea 4:6 (KJV)

Red Flag #2: Traps

I was very involved in Church activities and was being mentored by the elders. I would say I was their prized possession, so to speak. They wanted the best for me and checked up on me regularly.

Just about the time that was recommended for Bible School and had signed up the application forms, various young men started coming around, one after the other, showing interest in me; but the one that grabbed my attention was Denton (not his real name).

He and my adopted/spiritual mother, however, didn't hit it off too well on their first meeting. I realise now it is wise to trust motherly instincts. Believe me, mother knows best.

Our friendship grew rapidly. I deferred going to Bible School. I started avoiding my adopted mom and I stopped calling her; I even stopped going to Church. I was blinded by what seemed to be "LOVE". I allowed myself to be sidetracked.

Hazel-Ann Pariag

There is no doubt that distractions can come in many ways.

The snare is laid for him in the ground, and a trap for him in the way. Job 18:10

And this I speak for your own profit; not that I may cast a snare upon you, but for that which is comely, and that ye may attend upon the Lord without distraction. 1 Corinthians 7:35.

Satan uses people to set traps to take us into captivity. He places concealed traps along our path. It is vital that we learn to recognize these traps. It is only by discerning and studying the devices of our spiritual enemy that we can become alert to his strategies.

Anything that takes us out of God's presence is a recipe for disaster. Anything and anyone, we put before God is an idol, even if it's ourselves. This is called idolatry. Matthew 6:19-21 advises: ***"Lay not up treasures for yourselves upon earth, where moth and rust doth corrupt, and where thieves break through and steal. But lay up for yourselves treasures in Heaven, where neither moth nor rust doth corrupt, and where thieves do not break through nor steal: For where your treasures is, there will your heart be also."***

As God Almighty warned the children of Israel, *"I am the LORD your God, who brought you out of Egypt, out of the land of slavery. You shall have no other gods before me."* (Exodus 20:2-3)

Our attention often focuses on what's important to us, not on God's will. We need to choose the better way as Mary did and not become distracted as Martha was.

Luke 10:41-42 *"Martha, Martha," the Lord answered, "you are worried and upset about many things, but few things are needed—or indeed only one. Mary has chosen what is better, and it will not be taken away from her."*

Red Flag #3: Obsessive Shadowing

As the relationship progressed, he started running away from work to spend the time with me. My job often took me out of the office, as I am into transportation.

He worked from 6 a.m. - 2 p.m., but by 8 o'clock most mornings he was on my job and would stay with me until the end of my shift. If my shift was finished, and I was back at the office, he was also there. If I went to the hairdresser, he was there. My union held a march on behalf of our workers for an increase in salary, and he was also there, marching with me.

He became friends with all my friends and colleagues, and everything I did or anywhere I went he was also involved. This, I suppose, could be normal for young couples but it can also be an early sign of obsession and possessiveness.

Naïve as I was, I was happy, thinking he was madly in love with me and wanted to be in my company all day.

Hazel-Ann Pariag

He would escort me home, and we would remain talking late into the nights, making plans for our supposedly bright future together. Whenever it was late, we would agree that he would stay over, and sleep on the couch.

He lived in Central; I lived in the North and we both worked in the North, so sometimes sleeping over was convenient for him. Then he graduated from the couch to the bed, but we were cautious not to get intimate, acknowledging that that would be a sin.

These were all signs of domination, control and ownership, but I didn't recognise this then.

A friend of mine was told by the Holy Ghost some time ago: You are using the right key but for the wrong door. He came with all the right moves, but he was the wrong guy with wrong intentions. The devil knows how to set good traps, just as he did in the Garden of Eden. He sent out the bait, Eve took it and was hooked. She suffered the consequence and so do we. It was the same thing in my case; just different players - him and I.

1 Peter 5:8 warns, ***Be sober, be vigilant; the devil, as a roaring lion, walketh about, seeking whom He can devour.***

I would like to advise Christian women to remain in God's presence and carefully question if it is really God who has provided that answer, that man. Remember a woman must move from covering to covering; that is, from her father's covering to her husband's. Remember to guard your heart for it is what guides your judgement; neither should you walk away from your Source, for it is God who guides us.

Proverbs 4:23 advises, **Keep thy heart with all diligence, for out of it are the issues of life.**

Today, I ask myself: How could I believe that this apparent answer to prayer had come from my Father in heaven when I had walked away from Him at a time when I needed to get closer to Him for confirmation?

Red Flag #4: The Ex-Syndrome

When he met me, I was into catering, besides doing my regular job. With Christmas in the air, I was busy making cakes, pastelles, etc., for orders. As he was also a chef, we complemented each other well. "Unity is strength," I would say, as we got so much more done as a team.

One of his former girlfriends had ordered pastelles. I was at work when he notified me via a phone call that he was out grocery shopping with her for ingredients and he would be a bit late. I was not pleased, finding myself having to travel home alone, for the first time in six weeks. He showed up around 4:00 p.m., driving her vehicle. He informed me he had to return to pick her up at a friend's house, and then he was going to her house to make the pastelles.

I immediately showed my disapproval. Why this special treatment for her? After all, all the other orders were being done at my home, by both of us! Why did he have to go to her house *alone* to make them? That was our first argument.

He proceeded to soft-soap me, asking me if I didn't trust him and gave me all the sugar-coated reasons why I should not feel insecure, and promised he would be back by 8:00 p.m. When he did return, it was after 12:00 a.m. I was furious! I asked him how much he was paid. He confessed that he did not charge her because he had always done all her Christmas orders before. He brought me two pastelles to taste which I refused, of course!

I suggested that we call off the relationship because I was not going to be second-fiddle to anyone. His response to this was bribes and throwing pity parties. Then, apparently, he phoned her, informing her that I was not pleased, and that he would not be able to come to her house again because we were planning to settle down.

He even accused me of having him be the one fighting for the relationship! Now, I realise he was using reverse psychology on me and it succeeded in taking me on a guilt trip. I fell for it.

If a house is divided against itself, that house cannot stand. Mark 3:25

Proverbs 26:25-26 advises, **"When he speaks graciously, believe him not, for there are seven abominations in his heart; though his hatred be covered with deception, his wickedness will be exposed in the assembly."**

Many persons who are double-faced will say nice things to you, but behind your back, they will speak ill of you. Someone that is deceitful can't be trusted so when they speak graciously about you or someone you know, be on the alert. Their true hatred is really being hidden under deception and in time, their true intentions will be exposed.

It is so easy to deceive ourselves or be deceived by someone. One way to avoid being deceived is to be in the word of God daily. The best way to discern truth from error is to be reading the truth and that is to be found only in the Holy Bible.

Red Flag #5: Moving In

I moved in with him on January 11, 2012.

I was nagged incessantly about why it would be better to move to his house. We had numerous discussions about how much more economical it would be. After all, I was paying rent for a fully furnished two-bedroom apartment and he was paying a mortgage for a three-bedroom townhouse which had a stove, a three-piece living room set, a deep freeze, a bed and a dining set. But, if we got together and pooled our funds, this would also allow us to accumulate money for our wedding even quicker, he suggested.

Back then, I did not remember the wisdom of Romans 14:16: ***Let not your good be evil spoken of,*** and so I finally agreed. After all, on and off, he was practically living at my apartment. Now I was officially moving into his house. I started feeling guilty about this, but I justified my actions because we were soon going to be married.

Red Flags: Don't Ignore Them

I had a lot of mixed feelings, but I allowed carnal thinking and the enemy to play tricks with my mind. I kept thinking that I was not getting any younger and that my biological clock was ticking away.

I convinced myself that this was the answer to my prayers. I reasoned this was a God-sent opportunity, not to be missed. (Looking back, I can see where these were all lies of the enemy.) Besides, I liked him, and he was what many would call "husband-material" - an eligible bachelor, a keepsake!

When we met, I had no loans, now, after moving in with him, I had instalments to pay because I had upgraded from a twin tub to a heavy-duty washer to save myself energy as he was in the military and those uniforms were heavy! I also invested in a double-door refrigerator since the little one I had was like a dot in that big kitchen.

God does not set us up emotionally; we are the ones who complicate our lives. So, because of my disobedience, I now found myself in a situation where it seemed better to work with it than to walk away from it to save face.

As 2 Corinthians 6:14 so wisely points out: ***Do not be unequally yoked with unbelievers. For what do righteousness and wickedness have in common? Or what fellowship can light have with darkness?***

Hazel-Ann Pariag

RED FLAG WARNING ISSUED

Red Flag #6: Skeletons Coming Out of the Closet

The very next morning after I moved in, a female neighbour came across. She walked straight in and he greeted her. He introduced her with: "This is my neighbour." I said, "Hi, good morning.' She responded, "You had me worried about my neighbour. Ah wasn't seeing him at all.'

That sent my blood boiling. I stood there thinking: Even if you haven't seen him you could have said something like, "Hi, pleased to meet you. I now understand why I was not seeing him," or something to that effect!

This neighbour soon began to be a pest. After a while, I realised that many times he would disappear without saying a word, then I would see him popping out of her house. Obviously, I was not going to tolerate this much longer. I told myself this had to stop. It almost ended up being a catfight between us.

I am normally a mannerly and friendly person, so true to myself, I would greet my neighbours. He scolded me and told not to speak to anyone on the street. He had previous issues with most of them or they had issues with him. It seems there had been other women living with him in his home before me. I only found this out later.

I remembered seeing some female clothing in a barrel in one of the bedrooms, and when I enquired about it, he said they belonged to his mother, who was living in England.

Luke 8:17, **For there is nothing hidden that will not be disclosed, and nothing concealed that will not be known or brought out in the open.**

Red Flag #7: Financial Issues

On arriving home one evening from work, there was a letter under the door. He told me to open it. It was a Red Letter from the Housing Development Corporation (HDC) stating that he was in arrears of the sum of $30,000 and that it was the final notice for payment.

Then, all the other bills followed, including water and electricity, all due for disconnection notices. There I was asking myself what was he doing with his money all along? Why were the bills not being paid? His response was: No time off from work. He gave me his bank card and pin number to make the payments.

I could have fainted when after pushing the card into the ATM, I retrieved a receipt showing a balance of less than $10.00. When I confronted him, he said money would be in the account at the end of the month.

When month-end came, I suggested that we visit the HDC. We did so and an agreement was made to start paying extra to the fixed instalment to help clear off the outstanding arrears. I took my first loan from the Credit Union to assist with the other bills.

A man is supposed to provide for his family because that's how God designed it; at least, that's what I thought. Now, having given up my apartment, I had to channel *my* finances to assist in clearing his debts to save the roof over our heads and to take the shame out of my face. In all honesty, I was telling myself, "We're going to be in this all the way, anyhow, since it's a lifetime commitment."

Having removed myself from God's protection, I ran, jumped and skipped after my own pleasure, my own purpose and my earthly desires, and so I was now exposed to the enemy's devices, to the cankerworms which would eat up my finances and everything that I had worked so hard for.

Hazel-Ann Pariag

James 4:2-5 says, *Ye lust, and have not: ye kill, and desire to have, and cannot obtain: ye fight and war, yet ye have not, because ye ask not. Ye ask, and receive not, because ye ask amiss, that ye may consume it upon your lusts.*

In other words, we cannot ask for something that we're lusting after, and that's not in alignment with God's righteousness.

Joel 2:25 (NLT) *The Lord says, "I will give you back what you lost to the swarming locusts, and hopping locusts, the stripping locusts, and the cutting locusts. It was I who sent this great destroying army against you."*

Thankfully, when we come to our senses and seek God's way, there is the hope that we can redeem what the cankerworms have eaten.

Red Flag #8: Siblings and In-Laws

When I met my prospective in-laws, I found some of their behaviours acceptable and some I certainly was not accustomed to. Although generally, they lived lives I was uncomfortable with, I was a bit impressed with my choice of a future husband, and patted myself on the shoulder, for as far as I was concerned, he stood out from the rest. In fact, they looked up to him as their role model and mentor.

He, too, had serious, personal issues but, interestingly, they seemed unaware of this. Ironically, he was the most stable one. They were happy for him to have finally found a good woman to marry, so wedding plans were on the tip of everyone's tongue.

Red Flags: Don't Ignore Them

I had mixed feelings since I was going to marry into a family, where none could help the other spiritually. In fact, all were unmarried, co-habiting and living in sin. One relative had a child with a cousin which, we know, is incest. I felt somewhat trapped, but after speaking to him we came up with a plan to set the pace and be examples to his siblings. After all, we understood that God is able to deliver as long as we yield to His will and word.

Let your light so shine before men, that they may see your good works, and glorify your Father which is in Heaven. Matthew 5:16(KJV)

[God] will have all men to be saved, and to come unto the knowledge of truth. 1 Timothy 2:4(KJV)

Red Flag #9: Refusing Counsel

Time was going, and wedding plans were well on the way. We were in the month of March, and the wedding date was set for June. We went to our Apostle because I insisted that we get some pre-marital counselling, only to hear we would have to change the date because the Apostle was going to be out of the country in June.

He responded angrily to this, saying we were two grown adults who knew what we wanted so we didn't need any counselling. He argued that everyone's house runs differently so no one could tell him how to run our house.

He insisted we get married elsewhere and come back to our home church afterwards. I had already tied myself up financially and otherwise, and fearful of the consequences of not agreeing with him and calling off the wedding, I felt I was left with no choice but to work along with his decision.

Whoever loves discipline loves knowledge, but whoever hates correction is stupid. Proverbs 12:1(NIV)

Because of my disobedience in the beginning, I now found myself in a situation where it seemed better to work with it than to walk away from it in order to save face.

Do not be unequally yoked with unbelievers. For what do righteousness and wickedness have in common? Or what fellowship can light have with darkness? 2 Corinthians 6:14

Red Flag #10: Colourful Lies

When we met, he said he had been divorced for thirteen years, and I believed him. With wedding arrangements in full swing, we needed to apply for the marriage license but every time I asked him for his divorce papers, his response was he had to collect them from his lawyer.

Eventually, the truth came out. What he deemed a little white lie was actually a big red flag! My most dreaded fear had now become a reality, slapping me in the middle of my face: He was still married! If the earth could have opened at that moment, I would have willingly jumped in.

Instead, I chose to calm down, speaking to myself: "Ok, Moressa, take a deep breath. Now, what's the next move?" Here we are in March, the wedding has been planned for June. He asked if I had a lawyer. Immediately, I dialled her number and gave him the phone to speak to her. She suggested that we visit her office the next day.

The lawyer informed us that it was not that bad after all since there had been thirteen years of separation. She guaranteed that if we started proceedings immediately, the Decree Nisi would be granted in time so we could proceed with our wedding as planned.

She requested a down payment, of course, to begin filing the application. He had no money, so there I was once again dipping my hand into my pocket to pay for his affairs and to save myself from embarrassment.

After leaving her office, I asked him why he had not spoken the truth upfront. He casually said it was just a little white lie and he did not know that our relationship would have developed to this stage.

And ye shall know the truth, and the truth shall set you free. John 8:32(KJV)

Red Flag #11: Sickness and More Lies

John 8:44(KJV)
Ye are of your father the devil, and the lusts of your father ye will do. He was a murderer from the beginning, and abode not in the truth, because there is no truth in him. When he speaketh a lie, he speaketh of his own: for he is a liar, and the father of it.

One of the things that a responsible couple should talk about is each other's medical issues, if there are any. A spouse needs to know in the event that there is an emergency or, if either person falls ill, then the other would know what to do or what to relate to the medical personnel concerning medications and medical history, etc.

This information can save unnecessary heartache, time, money, embarrassment, or one's very life. He hid his illnesses from me. I observed his behaviour and symptoms and I asked if he was diabetic but he denied this.

Red Flags: Don't Ignore Them

I became suspicious when I found a bag of needles, tablets and a CDAP prescription hidden in a drawer. I took them to the pharmacy only to have my suspicions confirmed. This was embarrassing, and I felt deeply hurt. Going to be married to a man with a chronic disease was not the issue, it was the way in which I found out.

As time went by, a lot of other complications came along with the disease which led me to do some thorough research on it. I want to advise that the correct thing to do is to inform your partner, giving him/her the choice to decide whether or not they want to live with your complications. Do not deceive them.

Do unto others as you would have them do unto you.
Luke 6:31(NIV)

This individual sadly has since lost his eyesight. ***But he was wounded for our transgressions, he was bruised for our iniquities: the chastisement of our peace was upon him; and with his stripes, we are healed.*** Isaiah 53:5(KJV)

Praise God, He is able to heal.

Red Flag #12: The Wedding

On June 24th, 2012, we were married.

Our wedding was very fancy, fabulous indeed. It was lights, cameras, action! It was like a fairy-tale - everything seemed perfect. We looked spectacular. Anyone on the outside looking on would have said, "What a perfect couple; a match made in heaven!"

We were married at a five-star hotel in the north of our beautiful island of Trinidad, in St Ann's to be exact. Both the wedding and reception were held at the venue. Our honeymoon was compliments of the hotel.

The actual ceremony was done by an in-house pastor from the Caribbean Union College (CUC), West Indies. You would recall that our Apostle from our home church was not going to be in the country, so we had to get someone else to officiate at the ceremony.

Red Flags: Don't Ignore Them

We were whisked off after the ceremony to the Waterfront for pictures, and the traditional wedding-drive through the heart of the capital, Port of Spain - capturing everyone's attention, along the way, then back to the hotel for the reception.

Now let me burst your bubble without your permission. Having a fancy Cinderella wedding, whether it be in your homeland or in Disneyland, does not, will not, and cannot give or guarantee you a happy marriage. We listened to Satan and we allowed ourselves to be fooled. This led to our own downfall.

Except the Lord build the house, they labour in vain that build it: except the Lord keep the City, the watchman waketh but in vain. Psalm 127:1(KJV)

Life After the Wedding

In spite of all the fancy trimmings and costly glitter, I experienced a catastrophic marriage.

It was a short-lived life with this individual and it seemed like a lifetime sentence.

It was a life I had to literally run from, for my safety and peace of mind.

It was a life that took me to numerous police stations to make reports, and to the magistrate courts.

It was a life where on one occasion I had to be placed in a safe house - I was like a refugee on the run.

It was a life in which I had to seek a Protection Order from the court.

It was a life in which my husband was arrested on numerous

occasions and taken before the court for domestic violence.

It was a life in which he was also arrested by the military where he was a serving member at that time and was ordered by his superiors to receive treatment and counselling by a very competent psychologist.

Today, I am thankful to Almighty God for life. I do not wish anyone, not even my worst enemy, to experience the inhumane torture I went through.

A Prenuptial Checklist

Hidden secrets are lies but half-truths are also lies.

All relationships should have total, complete honesty and openness. For a relationship to work, firstly, God must be in it. When God is in it, everything else would fall into place, even if there are misunderstandings.

But seek ye first the Kingdom of God, and his righteousness: and all these things shall be added unto you. Matthew 6:33(KJV)

In our local dialect, we say that teeth and tongue will clash but they have to agree to be able to live in the same mouth. Agree to disagree - it's about fighting against the enemy, definitely not fighting each other. Remember you will become one flesh, therefore you should be on the same team.

Following God's guidelines for marriage and practising them will result in a harmonious relationship. Get to know the individual. Spend time asking questions, create scenarios, insist on feedback, pray together. Decide who brings what to the table. Decide on a place of worship and where you would live. Joint ownership would prevent one party saying to the other: Get out, this house belongs to me.

Two must become one in everything.

Advice for the Starry-Eyed

Here is my advice to young men and women planning to build a relationship that would hopefully result in marriage:

1. Make sure you and your partner are equally yoked.
2. Do not settle for less than the best.
3. Please seek godly counsel.
4. Don't ignore the Red Flags - they are real and cannot be hidden.
5. Ask God to confirm with a sign, if need be.
6. Ask the Holy Spirit to expose the things that are hidden.
7. Marry a person who loves God more than you.

It is imperative to follow God's guidelines when choosing a life partner.

Although the bible has given grounds for divorce, let me say to you: God hates divorce.

Obedience to God's will helps us do the things that are pleasing to him.

Keep thy heart with all diligence; for out of it are the issues of life. Proverbs 4:23 (KJV)

Some Things to Consider or Avoid in Preparation for Marriage

1) Hectic Routines and Commitments

Many times, we get caught up in our pursuit of work, career, studies and business, to meet our basic needs. As a result, we have little or no time for church, for studying God's word, nor even for prayer.

Ephesians 5:15-16

¹⁵See then that ye walk circumspectly, not as fools, but as wise,
¹⁶Redeeming the time, because the days are evil.

Make the most of your time at home, whilst driving or travelling to pray, and to reflect on God and His word. Some of us are workaholics; we chase after careers and success for our fulfilment rather than seeking to please God. It is imperative for our soul's salvation that we build a relationship with Jesus, our Saviour and our Redeemer.

2) Everyday Worries and Stress

Our parents and psychology have taught us that our three basic needs are food, clothing and shelter. However, we can all recognise that in modern-day living, the list is, in fact, much longer.

We often pay more attention to fulfilling our list which can create much stress, and we end up not giving our undivided attention and heeding His good advice.

Matthew 6:25-30

[25]Therefore I say unto you, take no thought for your life, what ye shall eat, or what ye shall drink; nor yet for your body, what ye shall put on. Is not the life more than meat, and the body than raiment?

[26]Behold the fowls of the air: for they sow not, neither do they reap, nor gather into barns; yet your heavenly Father feedeth them. Are ye not much better than they?

[27]Which of you by taking thought can add one cubit unto his stature?

[28]And why take ye thought for raiment? Consider the lilies of the field, how they grow; they toil not, neither do they spin:

[29]And yet I say unto you, that even Solomon in all his glory was not arrayed like one of these.

[30]Wherefore, if God so clothe the grass of the field, which today is, and tomorrow is cast into the oven, shall he not much more clothe you, O ye of little faith?

3) Mistaking Lust for Love

Lust and love do not have an age limit, and both can distract us spiritually if we are not operating in God's will; we can get caught up in lusting after someone to our own hurt. When someone is interested in us only for our body, our money, our talents, our connections, etc., or what we can do for them, then that's lust, not love. Loving someone, on the other hand, means we are totally committed to seeking their best interest.

Developing our relationship with God helps us to make the distinction between lust and love.

The heart's desire of most single persons is to be married and quite likely to have a fantasy wedding. We may see all our friends and relatives around us getting married, and feel we are being left out.

Even peer pressure from the married ones may lead us to the longing to be married; so, for some, it may seem like the in-thing to do. Feeling pressured to be married can be a huge distraction and not in harmony with God's will and purpose for our life.

Do not marry because of peer pressure and certainly, do not mistake lust for love.

Romans 12:2

²And be not conformed to this world: but be ye transformed by the renewing of your mind, that ye may prove what is that good, and acceptable, and perfect, will of God.

4) Social Media / Entertainment

Ah-ha! Which would you choose? Church on Sunday or the best movie in town, or on TV; or a football or cricket match at the Stadium? There is nothing wrong with having some form of entertainment but if we allow it to come in the way of our faith, that's when it becomes a distraction. We should never allow the enemy to persuade or pressure us to make a choice between entertainment and God.

Matthew 6:33

³³But seek ye first the kingdom of God, and his righteousness; and all these things shall be added unto you.

5) Self-appointed Ministry or Service

We can be distracted by some things we are sincerely doing in our desire to please Jesus. They may be good things, but Jesus does not want us to be doing these things at the expense of our relationship with him. What we do for Him must bring glory to Him and His kingdom.

Jesus frequently went off by himself to a quiet place to enjoy fellowship with his Father. He beckons us to do the same because there is fullness of joy in His presence and endless pleasure at His right hand.

Psalm 16:11

Thou wilt shew me the path of life: in thy presence is fullness of joy; at thy right hand there are pleasures for evermore.

6) Addictions

Many of us have addictions: those things that give us a 'high', that we can't seem to do without, that we must have. Some are visible, some hidden, some we acknowledge, some we deny and some we are not even aware of.

Distractions often indicate disconnection. Disconnection makes it easy to become enslaved to addictions. Instead of trusting and being totally dependent on God, one may rely on some narcotic substance, a vice, food or person to satisfy an inner void. That void is there because we have not recognised that it is only Our Heavenly Father who can fill it with HIS love through Jesus Christ.

We then become a victim to the trap and lies of addiction, which is really a snare of the enemy.

Some persons can become dependent on any of these:

music, movies, smartphones, games, people, sex, drugs and alcohol or cigarettes. None of these can ever satisfy us the way a committed relationship to Jesus Christ can!

7) The Me, Myself and I 'Sin-drome'

Many times, we become more focused on ourselves than on God. We separate ourselves from Him and drift spiritually, inflating our egos, leaning on our own understanding rather than on God's love for us. We need to fuel our faith and trust in God. It is not about us at all, no matter how talented and gifted we may be.

Proverbs 3:5-6

⁵Trust in the LORD with all thine heart; and lean not unto thine own understanding.
⁶In all thy ways acknowledge him, and he shall direct thy paths.

We are by nature sinful and selfish, and if we live led by that sinful nature, we will not build a relationship with Jesus, the One who knows us best and desires the best for us. After all, He asks that we give up this misguided self we wish to keep and follow Him who is the Way, the Truth and the Life. Trusting in Him brings us peace and helps us resolve the inner struggles we are so prone to have.

Romans 7:15-20

¹⁵For that which I do I allow not: for what I would, that do I not; but what I hate, that do I.

¹⁶If then I do that which I would not, I consent unto the law that it is good.

¹⁷Now then it is no more I that do it, but sin that dwelleth in me.

¹⁸For I know that in me (that is, in my flesh,) dwelleth no good thing: for to will is present with me; but how to perform that which is good I find not.

¹⁹For the good that I would I do not: but the evil which I would not, that I do.

²⁰Now if I do that I would not, it is no more I that do it, but sin that dwelleth in me.

We need to allow God to search our hearts and purify it. It is an ongoing struggle to keep our eyes focused on the King of Kings, but we should try, even harder, not to be distracted by the things of the world and stick to our resolution.

Sometimes the lack of money and the stress that comes with it can be a major distraction. When money becomes a constant focus (whether we have it or not), we lose faith in God and the gifts He provides.

Question to Self

Are there any worldly distractions I need to repent and put aside, in order to seek the Lord?

I have learnt to disassociate myself from the world's counterfeit peace, joy, strength and security. I now depend on God's peace and joy. I am resting God, enjoying His mercy and grace. When everything around me is shaking, my confidence and hope in Him remains.

Isaiah 30:15

¹⁵For thus saith the Lord GOD, the Holy One of Israel; In returning and rest shall ye be saved; in quietness and in confidence shall be your strength.

Isaiah 26:3

³Thou wilt keep him in perfect peace, whose mind is stayed on thee: because he trusteth in thee.

My Support Group

There are several people who assisted me in different ways throughout my marital ordeal - a time when I felt I existed in a torture chamber. I would have benefitted either from their prayers, a word of encouragement, a meal or even a temporary place to rest when I needed it. I thank God for putting them in place to help me keep my sanity. Indeed, it is promised: *When your mother and father forsake you, the Lord will take you up* (Psalm 27:10).

Very special thanks are due to Apostle Jemma Duncan with whom I shared my ordeal. Ninety-nine per cent of the time her response was: "Let God fight your battles. He can and will do a job better than you."

Pastor Ingrid Celestine was, and still is, always a phone call or text away. I say with gratitude: she is the mother who did not give birth to me.

These two mighty women of God helped me maintain my sanity.

Thank you, God.

Hazel-Ann Pariag

Red Flags: Don't Ignore Them

I want to acknowledge with deep gratitude:

Apostles Vivian and Jemma Duncan

Pastor Ingrid Celestine and family

Pastor Kenneth Caraby and family

Pastor Gillian Britto and Groans to Glory Ministry/ Wives on the Warpath

Retired WO1, Sgt Major Kenneth Doldron

Wayne and Wendy Elcock

Leiza Thompson

Hayden Whiskey

Arlene Lewis

Dana Charles

Ira Alexander and family

Gary Camejo

and

Madienne Mahon

Conclusion

I made some bad choices. I acted on my own and not with the guidance of the Holy Spirit. This resulted in my being subjected to all types of abuse: mental, emotional, spiritual, financial, psychological, verbal, and even some physical abuse.

What was supposed to be a marital home became a torture chamber.

Trust in the Lord with all your heart and lean not on your own understanding. Proverbs 3:5(NIV)

At the end of the day, disobedience to Almighty God landed me in a very heartbreaking situation. Although I had to literally remove myself from the situation, I am still living out the unfortunate consequences. I am still financially burdened, having to pay off outstanding bills on my own since the man I had married has now retired and is ailing with various medical complications, including the loss of his sight.

This is but Part One of my story. I promise in the sequel to be more detailed and in-depth.

I hope reading this book was of great assistance to those who are seeking a marriage partner or have intentions of doing so. I beseech you to reconsider doing it your way and that you do it God's way instead. It's really the best way.

Make Jesus Christ the foundation on which you build your home and marriage.

Psalm 127:1

1 Except the LORD build the house, they labour in vain that build it: except the LORD keep the city, the watchman waketh but in vain.

I appeal to you: Let Holy Spirit be your best friend; listen to him and not to your emotions. Get into your prayer closet and speak with Him; shut down or get away from all the noises and all the distractions.

Even if you are getting older and all your friends and siblings are getting married, PLEASE wait on God - Father knows best. Your sanity, and even your life depends on it.

It will prevent the pain and hurt of domestic abuse, violence and maybe even divorce.

Psalm 18:2

²The LORD is my rock, and my fortress, and my deliverer; my God, my strength, in whom I will trust; my buckler, and the horn of my salvation, and my high tower.

As I close this part of my story, I wish to share a quote I saw on Facebook with which I identify:

The road I have travelled has not always been an easy one and the path was often full of stones, but I am still here. I know that the only reason I was able to make it this far, the only reason I am still here today is due to the fact that God was walking the road with me every step of the way. **(God Memes, https://me.me)**

Volume 1 is what I call the smoke; the fire comes behind in Volume 2. Stay tuned.

GOD BLESS YOU

Contact Hazel-Ann Pariag

Email: hazel-annfullhundred1@live.com

*Available worldwide from Amazon
and all good bookstores*

---

http://mtp.agency

http://facebook.com/mtp.agency

@mtp_agency

www.ingramcontent.com/pod-product-compliance
Lightning Source LLC
LaVergne TN
LVHW020432080526
838202LV00055B/5144